THENOT & COLINET

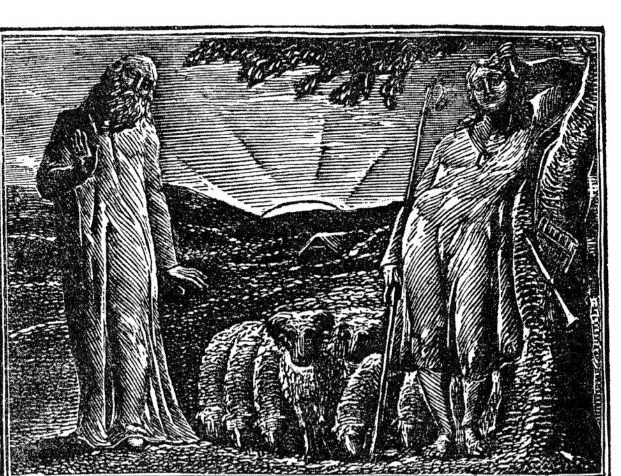

Thenot and Colinet

ILLUSTRATIONS TO THORNTON'S *PASTORALS OF VIRGIL*

William Blake

PALLAS 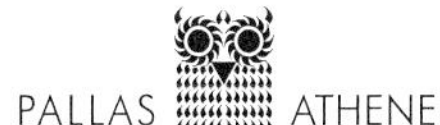 ATHENE

THENOT AND COLINET.

The Illustrations of this English Pastoral are by the famous Blake, the illustrator of *Young's* Night Thoughts, and *Blair's* Grave; who designed and engraved them himself. This is mentioned, as they display less of art than genius, and are much admired by some eminent painters.

THROUGH THE INTERVENTION of his last major patron, the painter John Linnell, Blake was commissioned in around 1821 to produce a set of illustrations for a schoolbook edition of the *Pastorals* of Virgil, as reimagined by the early eighteenth-century poet Ambrose Philips (whose nickname gave us the word 'namby-pamby'). They are Blake's only wood-engravings. The publisher-editor, Dr. Thornton, was unhappy with the roughness of Blake's images, and was in the process of having the blocks recut, until he was persuaded to reconsider by the protests of Linnell, together with those of the painters James Ward and Sir Thomas Lawrence. Thornton's own doubts are expressed by the disclaimer he printed under the frontispiece to the set (opposite). The engravings became Blake's most influential work, much admired by artists from Palmer onwards. They are reproduced here at their original size.

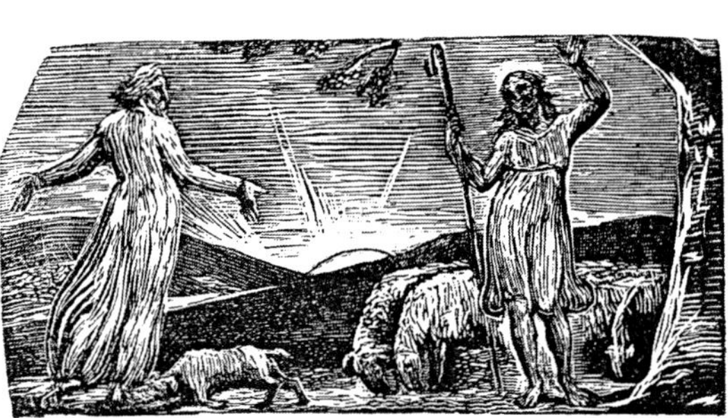

Thenot and Colinet

THENOT

Why do thy cloudy Looks thus melt in Tears
Unseemly, now all Heav'n so blithe appears?
Why in this mournful manner art thou found,
Unthankful Lad, when all things smile around?
Hark how the Lark and Linnet jointly sing,
Their Notes Soft-warbling to the gladsom Spring.

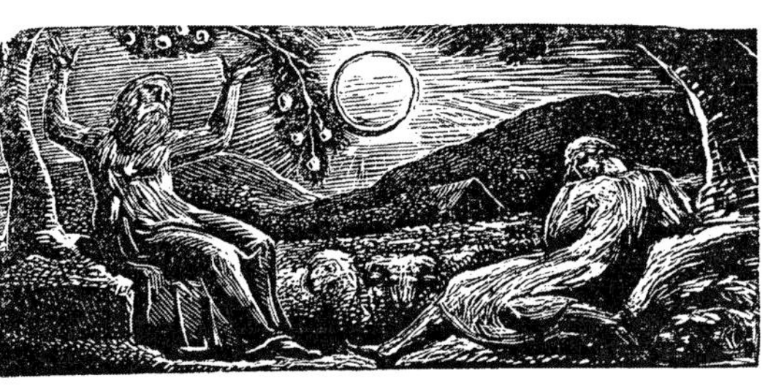

COLINET

Tho' soft their Notes, not so my wayward Fate,
Nor Lark would sing, nor Linnet in my State:
Each Creature to his proper Task is born;
As they to Mirth and Musick, I to mourn:
Waking at Midnight I my Woes renew,
And with my Tears increase the falling Dew.

THENOT

Can lusty Youth have Reason to complain?
Or who the Weight of Age cou'd e'er sustain,

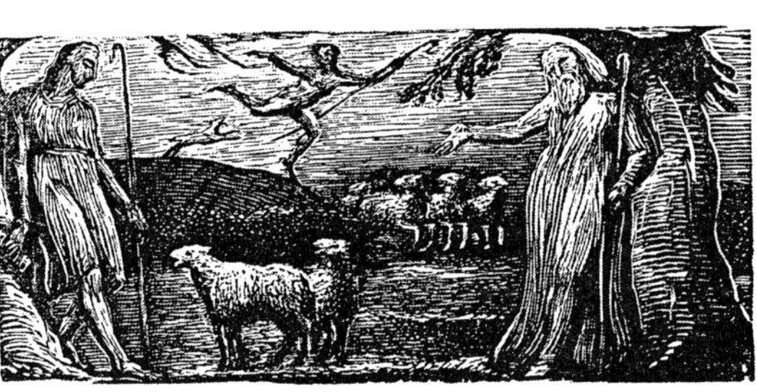

If, as our waning Forces daily cease,
The tiresome Burthen doubles its Increase?
Yet, tho' with Years my Body downward tend,
As Trees beneath their Fruit in Autumn bend,
My Mind a chearful Temper still retains,
Spite of my snowy Head and icy Veins:
For why shou'd Man at cross Mis-haps repine,
Sour all his Sweet, and mix with Tears his Wine?
But speak, for much it may relieve thy Woe,
To let a Friend thy inward Ailment know.

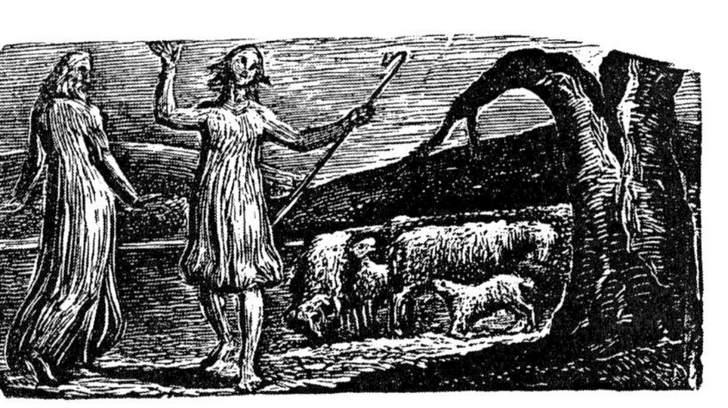

COLINET

'Twill idly waste thee, Thenot, a whole Day,
Should'st thou give Ear to all my Grief can say:
Thy Ews will wander, and thy heedless Lambs
With Bleatings loud require their absent Dams.

THENOT

There's Lightfoot, he shall tend them close, and I
'Twixt whiles a-cross the Plain will glance mine Eye.

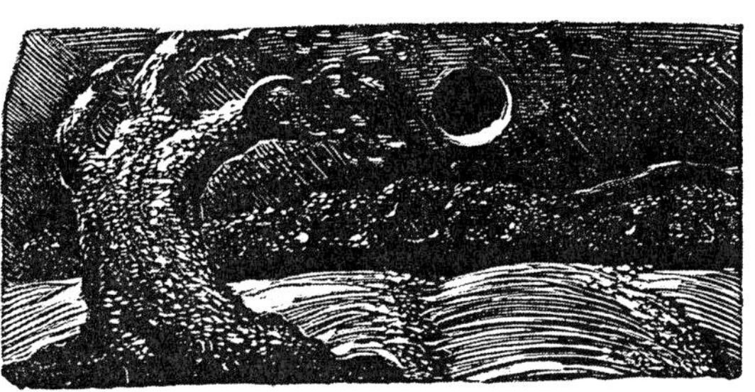

COLINET

Where to begin I know not, where to end,
Scarce does one smiling Hour my Youth attend:
Tho' few my Days, as my own Follies show,
Yet all those Days are clouded o'er with Woe:
No Gleam of happy Sun-shine does appear
My lowring Skie and wintry Days to chear.
My piteous Plight in yonder naked Tree,
That bears the Thunder-scar, too well I see;
Quite destitute it stands of Shelter kind,
The Mark of Storms, and Sport of ev'ry Wind:

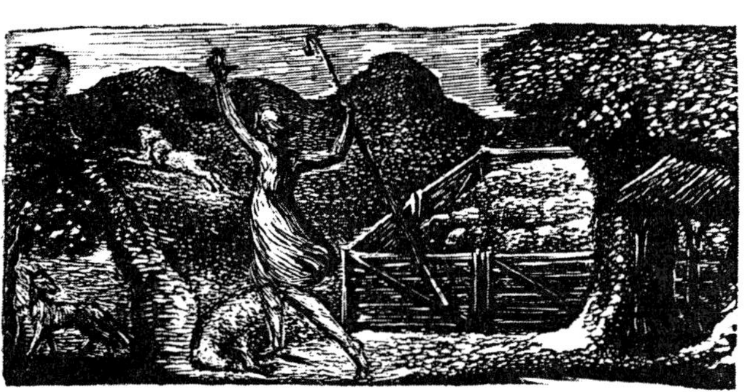

Its riven Trunk feels not th' Approach of Spring,
Nor any Birds among the Branches sing;
No more beneath thy Shade shall Shepherds throng
With merry Tale, or Pipe, or pleasant Song:
Unhappy Tree! and more unhappy I!
From thee, from me alike the Shepherds fly.

THENOT

Sure thou in some ill-chosen Hour wast born,
When blighting Mildews spoil the rising Corn,
Or when the Moon, by Witchcraft charm'd, fore-shows

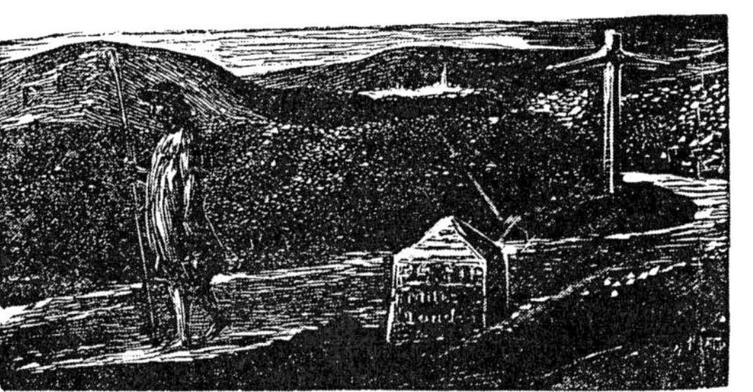

Thro' sad Eclipse a various Train of Woes:
Untimely born, ill Luck betides thee still.

COLINET

And can there, Thenot, be a greater Ill?

THENOT

Nor Wolf, nor Fox, nor rot amongst our Sheep;
For, from all these good Shepherd's Care may keep:
Against ill Luck all cunning Foresight fails;
Whether we sleep or wake it naught avails,

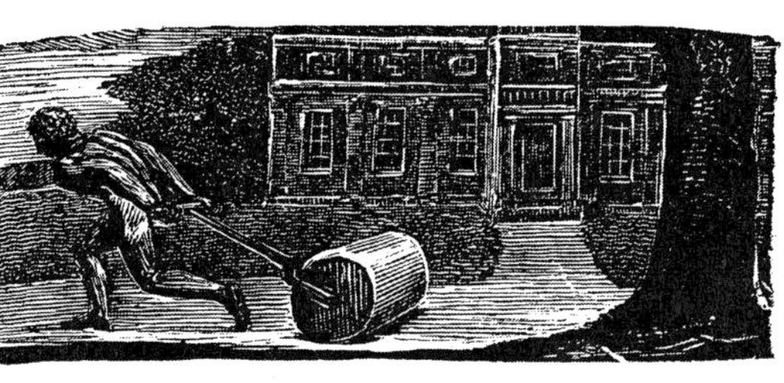

COLINET

Ah me, the while! ah me, the luckless Day!
Ah luckless Lad! the rather might I say:
Unhappy Hour, when first, in youthful Bud,
I left the fair Sabrina's silver Flood!
Ah silly I! more silly than my Sheep,
Which on thy flowry Banks I once did keep:
Sweet are thy Banks! O when shall I once more
With longing Eyes review thy beauteous Shore?
When in the Crystal of thy Waters see
My Face grown wan thro' Care and Misery?

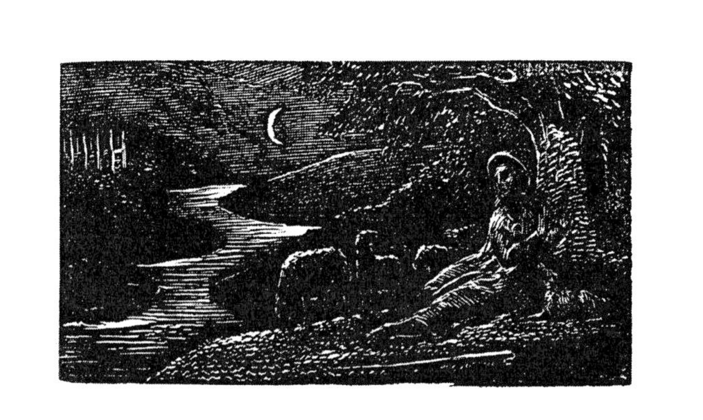

When shall I see my Hut, the small Abode
My self had rais'd and cover'd o'er with Clod?
Tho' small it be, a mean and humble Cell,
Yet was there room for Peace and me to dwell.

THENOT

And what the Cause that drew thee first away?
From thy lov'd Home what tempted thee to stray?

COLINET

A lewd Desire strange Lands and Swains to know;

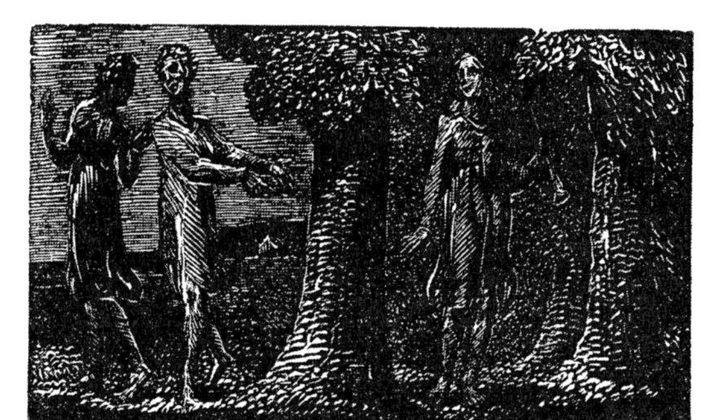

Ah God, that ever I shou'd covet Woe!
With wandring Feet unblest, and fond of Fame,
I sought I know not what, besides a Name.

THENOT

Or, sooth to say, didst thou not hither roam
In hopes of Wealth, thou could'st not find at home?
A rowling Stone is ever bare of Moss;
And to their Cost green Years old Proverbs cross.

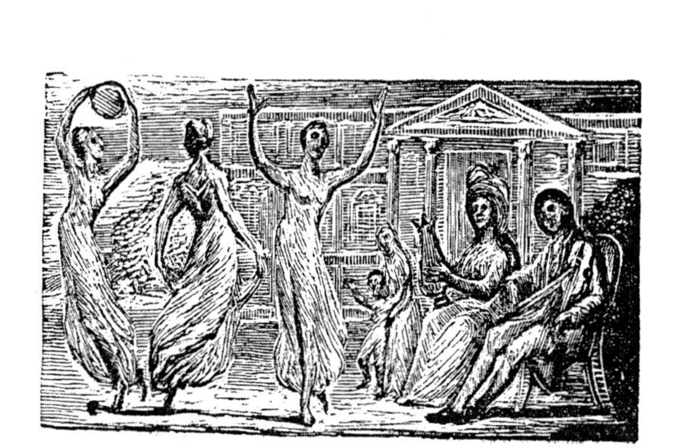

COLINET

Small need there was, in flatt'ring Hopes of Gain,
To drive my pining Flock a-thwart the Plain
To distant Cam; fine Gain at length, I trow,
To hoard up to my self such deal of Woe!
My sheep quite spent through Travel and ill Fare,
And, like their Keeper, ragged grown and bare;
Here on cold Earth to make my nightly Bed,
And on a bending Willow rest my Head.
'Tis hard to bear the pinching Cold with Pain;
And hard is Want to th' unexperienc'd Swain:

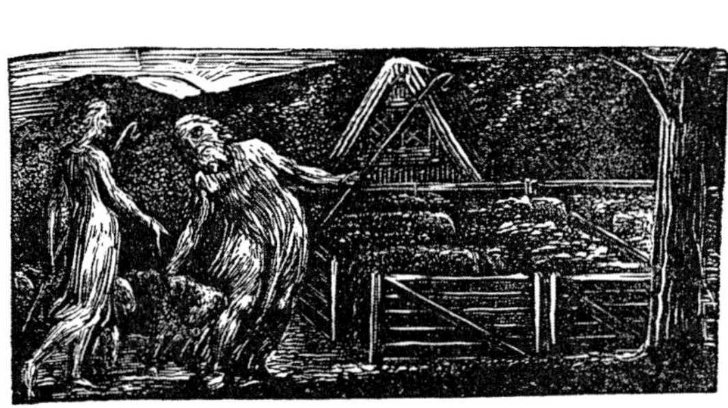

But neither Want nor pinching Cold is hard,
To blasting Storms of Calumny compar'd:
Unkind as Hail it falls, whose pelting Show'rs
Destroy the tender Herb and budding Flow'rs.

THENOT

Slander we Shepherds count the greatest Wrong;
For, what wounds sorer than an evil Tongue?

COLINET

Untoward Lads, that Pleasance take in spite,

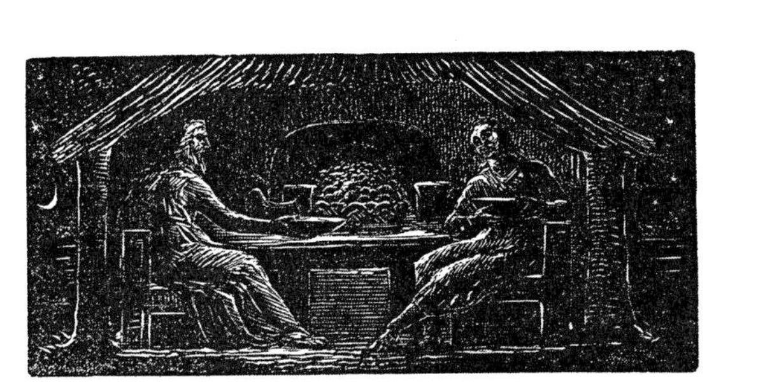

Make mock of all the Ditties I indite.
In vain, O Colinet, thy Pipe so shrill
Charms ev'ry Vale, and gladdens ev'ry Hill;
In vain thou seek'st the Cov'rings of the Grove,
In the cool Shade to sing the Heats of Love;
No Passion, but rank Envy, canst thou move:
Sing what thou wilt, ill Nature will prevail,
And ev'ry Elf has Skill enough to rail.
But yet, tho' poor and artless is my Vein,
Menalcas seems to like my simple Strain;
And long as he is pleas'd to hear my Song,

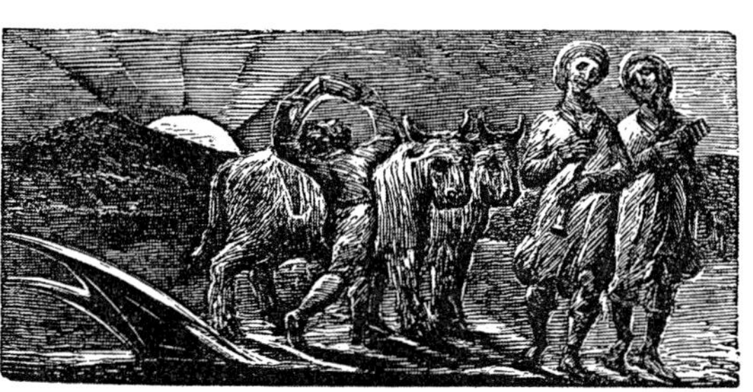

Which to Menalcas does of Right belong,
Nor Night nor Day shall my rude Musick cease,
I ask no more, so I Menalcas please.

THENOT

Menalcas, Lord of all the neighb'ring Plains,
Preserves the Sheep, and o'er the Shepherds reigns:
For him our yearly Wakes and Feasts we hold,
And chuse the fattest Firstlings from the Fold:
He good to all, that good deserve, shall give
Thy Flock to feed, and thee at Ease to live;

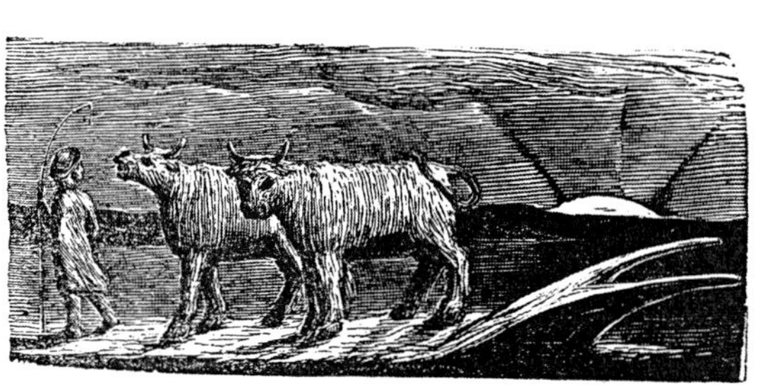

Shall curb the Malice of unbridled Tongues,
And bounteously reward thy rural Songs.
This Night thy Cares with me forget, and fold
Thy Flock with mine to ward th' injurious Cold.
Sweet Milk and clouted Cream, soft Cheese and Curd,
With some remaining Fruit of last Year's Hoard,
Shall be our Ev'ning Fare; and for the Night,
Sweet Herbs and Moss, that gentle Sleep invite.
And now behold the Sun's departing Ray
O'er yonder Hill, the sign of ebbing Day:
With Songs the jovial Hines return from Plow,
And th' unyok'd Heifers, pacing homeward, low.

First published 2019 by
PALLAS ATHENE (PUBLISHERS) LIMITED
2 Birch Close,
Hargrave Park,
London N19 5XD
www.pallasathene.co.uk
Revised and reprinted 2024

ISBN 978 1 84368 192 2

Printed in England

SERIES EDITOR
Alexander Fyjis-Walker
EDITORIAL ASSISTANTS
Patrick Davies and Joshua Hunter